"PACEM IN TERRIS"

Summary & Commentary for the
50th Anniversary of the Famous Encyclical Letter
of Pope John XXIII on World Peace

JOE HOLLAND

President, Pacem in Terris Global Leadership Initiative
Washington DC
Professor of Philosophy & Religion, St. Thomas University
Miami Gardens, Florida

Postmodern Catholic Social Teaching Series

Volume 1

PACEM IN TERRIS PRESS

www.paceminterris.net

This book is published with gratitude to
to Sr. Claudia Carlin and Pierian Press for earlier permission to use
papal quotations from Sr. Carlin's multivolume edited collection titled
THE PAPAL ENCYCLICALS.

The cover photo is taken from within
the gentle Southern Appalachian Mountains in Eastern Tennessee
at the site of the Narrow Ridge Earth Literacy Center.
The photo symbolizes the interrelationship of social "Peace on Earth"
with ecological "Peace with Earth"

This book was produced by Pacem in Terris Press
as a project of the Pacem in Terris Global Leadership Initiative

ISBN-13: 978-1479126347
ISBN-10: 1479126349

PACEM IN TERRIS PRESS
The Publishing Service of
Pax Romana / Cmica-usa
1025 Connecticut Avenue NW. Suite 1000
Washington DC 20036

"On Establishing Peace among All Peoples

in Truth, Justice, Love, and Liberty"

JOHN XXIII

(Subtitle of Pacem in Terris)

PACEM IN TERRIS BOOKS

Postmodern Ecological, Social, & Spiritual Thought
for the Emerging Global Civilization and the Emerging World Church

"PACEM IN TERRIS"
Summary & Commentary for the Famous Encyclical Letter
of Pope John XXIII on World Peace
(Postmodern Catholic Social Teaching Series, Volume 1)
Joe Holland, 2012

HUMANITY'S AFRICAN ROOTS
Remembering the Ancestors' Wisdom
Joe Holland, 2012

100 YEARS OF CATHOLIC SOCIAL TEACHING
DEFENDING WORKERS & THEIR UNIONS
Summaries & Commentaries for Five Landmark Papal Encyclicals
Joe Holland, 2012

THE "POISONED SPRING" OF ECONOMIC LIBERTARIANISM
Menger, Mises, Hayek, Rothbard: A Critique from
Catholic Social Teaching of the Austrian School of Economics
Angus Sibley, 2011

FORTHCOMING

THE PACEM IN TERRIS GLOBAL LEADERSHIP INITIATIVE
Reading the Signs of the Times for Society and Church
at the End of the Modern World
(Pacem in Terris Global Initiative Series, Volume 1)
Joe Holland, 2012

THE VISION OF JOHN XXIII
Prophetic Founder of Catholic Social Teaching for
the Postmodern Global Era, 1958-1963
(Postmodern Catholic Social Teaching Series, Volume 2)
Joe Holland, Projected for 2013

LABOR PRIESTS & THE CATHOLIC CHURCH
Labor Priests Series, Volume I
Rev. Patrick J. Sullivan, CSC, Projected for 2013

Scholars interested in submitting a related and well researched manuscript
to be considered for Publication by Pacem in Terris Press
should send an email of inquiry to paceminterris@comcast.net

EARLIER BOOKS BY JOE HOLLAND

HUMANITY'S AFRICAN ROOTS
Remembering the Ancestors' Wisdom
2012

BEYOND THE DEATH PENALTY
The Development in Catholic Social Teaching
Co-Editor Michael McCarron
2007

MODERN CATHOLIC SOCIAL TEACHING
The Popes Confront the Industrial Age, 1740-1958
2003

THE NEW DIALOGUE OF CIVILIZATIONS
Co-Editor Roza Pati
2003

"THE EARTH CHARTER"
A Study Book of Reflection for Action
Co-Author Elisabeth Ferrero
2002

VARIETIES OF POSTMODERN THEOLOGY
Co-Editors David Griffin & William Beardslee
1989

CREATIVE COMMUNION
Toward a Spirituality of Work
1989

AMERICAN AND CATHOLIC
The New Debate
Co-Editor Anne Barsanti
1988

VOCATION AND MISSION OF THE LAITY
Co-Author Robert Maxwell
1986

SOCIAL ANALYSIS
Linking Faith and Justice
Co-Author Peter J. Henriot, SJ
1980 & 1983

THE AMERICAN JOURNEY
A Theology in the Americas Working Paper
1976

This book is dedicated to the late

CÉSAR JEREZ, S.J.

Priest, Scholar, Prophet, & Friend

.

"The Spirit of the Lord is upon me;
therefore, he has anointed me.
He has sent me to bring glad tidings to the poor,
to proclaim liberty to captives,
recovery of sign to the blind
and release to prisoners,
to announce a year of favor from the Lord."

THE GOSPEL ACCORDING TO LUKE

CHAPTER 4, VERSES 18-19

TABLE OF CONTENTS

OPENING REFLECTION ON

THE ENCYCLICAL

T he year 2013 marks the 50ᵗʰ Anniversary of PACEM IN TERRIS (Peace on Earth), the landmark 1963 encyclical letter issued by Pope John XXIII (1958-1963) on world peace. Despite its age, this encyclical remains the most famous and relevant papal document of contemporary times. On the occasion of this Anniversary, and to help people understand this important document, the Pacem in Terris Global Leadership Initiative offers a summary of, and a commentary on, this most important document.

A crucial piece of historical background to the document is the role that Pope John reportedly played in the infamous 1962 "Cuban Missile Crisis," which placed the entire human family and all of life on Earth under imminent threat of a catastrophic thermonuclear war between the Soviet Union and the United States.

In his 1972 book THE IMPROBABLE TRIUMVIRATE: JOHN F. KENNEDY, POPE JOHN, NIKITA KHRUSHCHEV, the late Norman Cousins (formerly editor of THE SATURDAY REVIEW) reported the little known fact that Pope John played a secret but key role in resolving the Cuban Missile Crisis. In light of Cousin's revelations, it could be that, without Pope John's behind-the-scenes mediation, the eventual back-channel communications between Kennedy and Khrushchev might have failed, with horrendous consequences.

This experience must have had a tremendous impact on Pope John. Reportedly, it led to his preparing this his final encyclical, even though he was dying of cancer with only months to live.

Upon its publication, PACEM IN TERRIS was warmly received across the world. Some believe that it provided an important spiritual-intellectual contribution to ending the Cold War.

The vision that John laid out in this encyclical was an early prophetic call to create a humanistic-ecological path for what is now called "globalization." John's document is one of the early public recognitions of the emergence of the "world economy," which he then addressed by identifying the need for what today is called "global governance." In that regard, John celebrated and praised the United Nations Organization and its member agencies.

The encyclical is also notable in that it celebrates the end of Western *colonialism* and the emergence of *women* into public life, both of which John referred to as *signs of the times,* along with a third "sign," namely the political-economic emancipation of *workers.*

In addition, in this document a Catholic pope, for the first time in the Modern Era, embraced the human-rights tradition which arose from the Modern European Enlightenment, though John sought to establish for human rights a deeper and richer philosophical ground in Natural Law.

Again, this book is being published on the eve of the 50th anniversary year of PACEM IN TERRIS. The message of that document still challenges us, and John remains a prophetic visionary for his beloved Catholic Church and for his beloved human family.

INTRODUCTION

I n 1963, within the traumatic wake of the Cuban Missile Crisis, Pope John XXIII issued his most famous encyclical, PACEM IN TERRIS (Peace on Earth), carrying the subtitle *On Establishing Peace among All Peoples in Truth, Justice, Love, and Liberty.*[1] It was addressed to all the Catholic bishops, clergy, and faithful, and also for the first time for a papal encyclical to *all People of Good Will.*

When it was first issued, this encyclical received extraordinary public attention across the Catholic Church, in the world press, and at the United Nations. It continues to be celebrated today.

---

[1] Claudia Carlin, PAPAL ENCYCLICALS 1958-1981 (The Perian Press, 1990), pp. 107-129. The paragraph numbers used here are from the English version. For the headings in the document, however, I mostly use my own English translations from the Italian version, since presumably the Italian headings reflect the original intention of the reported Italian ghost-writer, Pietro Pavan. Also within this book, material in italics indicates a quotation from PACEM IN TERRIS.

For the subtitle, the official Italian version uses the Italian *Amore* for the Latin *Caritate,* and the Italian *Tutte le Genti* for the Latin *Omnium Gentium.* So for the subtitle here, I have translated *Caritate* as *Love* (rather than *Charity*) *and Omnium Genium* as *All Peoples* (rather than *Universal*). In the English language *Love* better reflects the meaning of the Latin *Caritas,* and *Universal* seems an inaccurate translation of *Omnium Gentium.* Note also that in its internal headings, the Italian version does not use the non-inclusive word "men," but refers inclusively to "human beings." (The Latin version has no internal headings.)

3

PACEM IN TERRIS is framed by an Introduction on *the order of the universe* and on *order among human beings,* and by a Conclusion on *the Prince of Peace.* After its Introduction, the document moves through five substantive sections addressing:

- *Order among Human Beings* [2]
- *Relationships between Human Beings & Public Authorities within Individual Political Communities*
- *Relationships among Political Communities*
- *Relationships of Human Beings & Political Communities within the Global Community*
- *Pastoral References*

At the end of each of the document's four major sections, John offers his reflection on the *Signs of the Times.* These additions reveal the *historical method* underlying the Johannine approach. Let us now examine the document itself.

Order in the Universe

John's Introduction opens with his *diligent observance of the divinely established order of the universe.* It states that God's own order prevails in Nature and that the progress of Science and Technology is revealing to us the *infinite greatness of God.* [3]

---

[2] The official English version renders this particular heading non-inclusively as *Order between Men.* But the Italian version renders it inclusively it as *L'Ordine tra Gli Esseri Umani* (Order among Human Beings). Again, the Italian version is presumably the original.

[3] Pars. 1-3.

John linked the human order with the Divine order by recalling that *God created humanity 'in his own image and likeness,' endowed it with intelligence and freedom, and made it the human lord of creation,* and that the order of creation is *revealed to humans by one's conscience.*[4]

Order among Human Beings

John continued his Introduction by lamenting that *there is a disunity among individuals and among nations which is in striking contrast to this perfect order in the universe,* such that it seems that human relationships are only *governed by force.* One reason for this disarray, he proposed, is the *erroneous opinion* that only blind elemental forces of the universe govern political relationships. On the contrary, he insisted, the laws of society are written in human nature.[5]

---

[4] Pars. 3.

[5] Pars. 4-7.

BACKGROUND PHILOSOPHICAL COMMENT

The Modern Philosophical-Scientific Appropriation of the Classical Materialist Cosmology of Epicurus

T hough not explained in the encyclical, John's reference to *erroneous opinions* was an implicit critique of the atomistic-mechanical Cosmology that early modern Philosophy and early modern Science had widely appropriated within the early modern rise of the "New Science".

Later, in the modern European Enlightenment, this atomistic-mechanical Cosmology was applied to modern Western political and economy theory, and more widely to all modern Western social theory.

This led to the false philosophical view that human persons are autonomous individuals completely separate from each other, with their relationship mediated only by negotiated contracts based on voluntaristic self-interest. In this perspective, human freedom is seen as a negative concept, as freedom from coercion, and without positive substantive meaning.

This atomistic-mechanical philosophy constitutes the *deep materialist Cosmological foundation of the modern Western bourgeois cultural project*, including its Liberal-Capitalist and Scientific-Socialist ideological expressions.

This materialist Cosmology was planted as the cultural basis of early modern Philosophy and early modern Science by what were then called "natural philosophers" (today called "scientists"). Its grounding articulation may be found in Cartesian Philosophy and Newtonian Physics (or "Mechanics").

These natural philosophers appropriated the atomistic-mechanical Cosmology from Renaissance translations of the classical Roman philosopher Lucretius' (c. 99-55 BCE) famous poem, DE RERUM NATURA, which praised the atomistic-mechanical Cosmology of the earlier Greek materialist philosopher Epicurus (341-270 BCE).

For Epicurus, matter was all that existed and it was made up of tiny indivisible "atoms" (*atoma*, meaning "uncuttable particles"), which were ultimately autonomous one from each other and moved only by blind force and random chance with no rational or spiritual meaning.

For Epicurus, philosophical Ethics meant the therapeutic attempt to withdraw from political life, to avoid marriage and family, and to try to live without emotional disturbance, hopefully minimizing bodily pain, but ideally with some modest pleasures.

There were "gods," Epicurus stated, but they were simply the material stars in the sky, and they cared only for their own selves with no concern for humans or the rest of the Cosmos. Meanwhile, for him religion was something evil – a source of fear and so to be rejected, though the unconcerned "gods" in the starry heavens might be publicly honored.

Without religion, he proposed, death need not be feared. For it simply meant decomposition of the "atoms" which had temporarily aggregated into our bodies and which was all there is.

Thus, for Epicureanism there is no order, purpose, or meaning to the Universe, except the material atoms of which things are temporarily and mechanically composed. And there is no point to human life except to try to avoid pain, to seek tranquility, perhaps to find a few modest pleasures, and ultimately without fear to accept death as the end of our meaningless identity.

As noted, the Epicurean Philosophy, after being appropriated cosmologically by early modern European natural philosophers, was then applied in the Modern European Enlightenment to what eventually became the Modern Human Sciences, beginning with Politics and Economics – first, in the *Liberal-Capitalist* ideology, and later in the *Scientific-Socialist* ideology.

Also, this development would take philosophical-ethical expression as modern *Utilitarianism*, though with an altruistic political concern not found in Epicurus. Again, the atomistic-mechanical Cosmovision of Epicurus became the philosophical foundation of the modern Western bourgeois cultural project in both of its reductionist-materialist ideologies.

For example, *Adam Smith* – the main founding philosopher of the modern ideology of Liberal Capitalism – appropriated from Isaac Newton the Epicurean atomistic-mechanical system as his own philosophical-scientific method for his liberal version of the Political Economy.

Similarly, *Karl Marx* – the main founding philosopher of the modern ideology of Scientific Socialism – wrote his doctoral dissertation on a comparison of the materialist philosophies of Democritus (an early atomist) and Epicurus, with greater praise for Epicurus. Marx then made Epicurean materialism the conceptual foundation for his Marxian version of the modern Political Economy.

In early Christian history, however, when the young Christian movement had intellectually engaged the Roman Empire, early Christian thinkers had rejected the Philosophy of Epicurus, since it preached materialism, rejected religion and family, and withdrew from social concern.

Instead, these Christian thinkers had appropriated major elements of the alternative Roman Stoic Philosophy which, like the earlier Greek Socratic philosophers (Socrates, Plato, and Aristotle) from whom it had sprung, found spiritual meaning and rational order and purpose in the Cosmos, all of which they saw as grounded in the Divine *Logos* (Word) revealed in all of creation.

This Stoic *Logos* tradition, as the main alternative to the Epicurean materialist *Chaos* tradition, had its earlier roots in the ancient Greek philosopher Heraclitus, and may have had still older Egyptian roots.

So it is not surprising that deep thinkers in both late Second-Temple Judaism and early Christianity were drawn within their Hellenistic environment to Stoic Philosophy. We see this with Paul's EPISTLE TO THE ROMANS and with the GOSPEL OF JOHN, in which the *Logos* (Word) becomes the name for God.

Thus, when the papal encyclicals critique the *errors* of modern Philosophy (again, as expressed in the modern Liberal-Capitalist and Scientific-Socialist ideologies), it is to this atomistic-mechanical Cosmology – with its reductionist, materialist, and now *utilitarian* Ethics – that they implicitly refer.[6]

It is important to note, however, that in the now emerging Postmodern Electronic Era (with its electronic microscopes, electronic telescopes, and electronically computerized data) the modern appropriation of Epicureanism as a grounding paradigm for Philosophy and Science is being superseded by a postmodern (and so post-Cartesian and post-Newtonian) "New Cosmology.".[7]

---

[6] For a scholarly and lyrical pro-Epicurean study of the influence of Epicurus' Philosophy on the conceptual foundations of the modern Science, see Catherine Wilson's beautifully written book, EPICUREANISM AT THE ORIGINS OF MODERNITY (Oxford UK: Clarendon Press, 2008). But Catherine Wilson's book also seems to suggest, at least to this reader, that deep within Epicurus – as evidenced by his awe before the creativity of nature and his devoted appreciation of the feminine – there may be found something deeper than pure materialism and chaotic chance. For another recent work reporting on the influence of Epicurus on early modern Science and early modernity overall, see also Stephen Greenblatt's pro-Epicurean and delightfully written book (though one marred by simplistic anti-Catholic prejudices), THE SWERVE: HOW THE WORLD BECAME MODERN (W.W. Norton & Co., 2012).

[7] There are rich resources for understanding the New Cosmology, but sharing them here is beyond the scope of this small book. A helpful starting point for understanding the "New Cosmology" is Brian Thomas Swimme & Mary Evelyn Tucker's profound book, JOURNEY OF THE UNIVERSE (New Haven: Yale University Press, 2011). There is also a companion video of the same name.

PART I

ORDER AMONG HUMAN BEINGS

I n Part I of his encyclical, John developed his first substantive section which addresses the theory of *human order*, and also of *human rights and human duties* within that order.

The center of this theory is the *human person* as intelligent and free, with rights and duties flowing from human nature and which, he proposed, are *universal, inviolable, and inalienable.*[8]

Further, John added, this fundamental human dignity is enhanced by our knowledge through Christian faith that humans have been made through the grace of Jesus Christ into *sons (and daughters) and friends of God and heirs to eternal glory.*[9]

Human Rights

Every Human Being is a Person, Subject of Rights and Duties

Here, John accepted the liberal human-rights tradition of the French Revolution, which until this point the Catholic popes had

---

[8] The Italian version inclusively refers to the human person as a "human being" *(essere umano)*, while the English version non-inclusively refers to "men."

[9] Pars. 8-10.

rejected because it had been grounded in the erroneous atomistic-mechanical Philosophy. John, however, integrated this secular human-rights tradition into the Natural Law theory of society, which (as noted earlier) the Catholic tradition had appropriated early on from the Roman Stoics, including the correlative theory of rights and duties, with all grounded in the *Logos* of Divine truth and order.

Next, John offered his summary statement of the main rights of his Catholic appropriation of the revolutionary liberal human-rights tradition. His summary merged the two United Nations covenants on human rights.[10]

Right to Existence & Decent Standard of Living

John began his summary of human rights with the *right to life* and the derivative rights of *bodily integrity*, including the means of human development like *food, clothing, shelter, and social services, including care in illness, disability and widowhood, and old age and forced unemployment.*[11]

Rights Regarding Moral & Cultural Values

Then John moved to *moral and cultural rights*. These include, he said, the right as a human person to respect and a good name and to the common good (within moral limits), as well as to freedom of speech and publication, to choice of profession, to freedom of

---

[10] Regarding these two covenants, see:
http://en.wikipedia.org/wiki/International_Covenant_on_Civil_and_Political_Right (accessed 2012-08-12).

[11] Par. 11.

14

information, and to cultural benefits like education and professional training, with advanced studies for the more gifted.[12]

Right to Worship God according to
Dictates of a Correct Conscience

Next, John affirmed the right to worship according a correct conscience, and he included the private and public profession of religion. He commented that *true freedom* (which he linked with a *correct conscience*) is that which safeguards the dignity of the human person.

Then he stated that this true freedom *has always been desired by the Church*, though historians might have problems with that claim.[13] While the Western tradition of personal freedom does indeed seem to have roots in the Christian tradition, and in part in the tradition of Catholicism's Canon Law, we also need to remember the past official Catholic support (with important exceptions) for torture, anti-Semitism, the Crusades, the Inquisition, the invasion and conquest of the First Nations of the Americas, and the Atlantic slave-system.

Much later, Pope John Paul II would ask forgiveness for many of these outrageous Catholic violations of human rights. But John XXIII did not refer to them.

---

[12] Pars. 12-13.

[13] Par. 14.

Right to Freedom in Choice of State in Life

John also included in his list the right to found a family, with women and men enjoying equal rights and duties, or alternately to embrace the priesthood or religious life (though not noting the male limitation of the Catholic priesthood), and for the family a right prior to the state to educate its children. In addition, he recalled the Catholic position that *the family is the natural, primary cell of human society.*[14]

Rights Pertaining to Economic World

Here John affirmed the *right to employment*, as well as to personal economic initiative, plus the derivative right of humane working conditions that include a proper responsibility in work, a just family wage, and private ownership, including productive property though with social obligation.[15]

Right of Assembly & Association``

Next, John listed the right of people to meet together and to form associations, including of persons acting on their own initiative and responsibility. He urgently encouraged *the founding of a great many such intermediate groups* (presumably including unions), all of which he saw as *essential for safeguarding ... personal freedom and dignity.*[16]

---

[14] Pars. 15-17.

[15] Pars. 18-22.

[16] Pars. 23-24.

Right of Emigration & Immigration

Next, John defended the right of freedom of movement within states and, when there are just reasons, between states. He pointed out that, even though one is a citizen of another state, one does not thereby loose one's *universal human rights,* for everyone carries a *universal citizenship* based on human dignity.[17]

Political Rights

John also defended the right of the human person to take an active part in public life and to contribute to society, as well as the right to legal protection for all human rights.[18]

As noted, in highlighting these individual rights John embraced the modern human-rights tradition, though he did not accept the assumption of the Modern European Enlightenment's atomistic-mechanical Cosmology, which provided its modern philosophical grounding.

Instead, he grounded these rights philosophically in the deeper, older, and socially oriented foundation of *Natural Law,* and also theologically in the Biblical teaching that human person is made in the *imago Dei* (image of God).

In the next part of this first section, John turned to the second half of the Catholic theory of the social order, namely the *social character of the human person* and the *duties* which flow from it.

---

[17] Par. 25.

[18] Par. 26-27.

Human Duties

Inseparable Relationship between Rights & Duties in the Same Person

John began his exploration of the *social character* of the human person by stating that all rights have *correlative duties*, with both rights and duties flowing from Natural Law. Such duties, he stated, were not only incumbent on the self (e.g., the right to life entails the duty to preserve one's life), but also on others (e.g., not to take the life of another).[19]

In an implicit critique of the modern Western cultural emphasis on rights but neglect of duties, he argued that to claim rights and to ignore their correlative duties would be *like building a house with one hand and tearing it down with the other.*[20]

In Modernity's underlying atomistic-mechanical philosophical-scientific Cosmology, Epicurean "atoms" have "freedom" when their blind movement is not impeded, and so no Epicurean "atom" has any responsibility (duty) to any other Epicurean "atom." Consequently, for the Modern Cosmology hypothetically autonomous humans (again, like Epicurean "atoms") seek "freedom" as the *individual rights* of self-interest without correlative *social duties.*

In Mutual Collaboration

John also rejected the modern Western individualist (again, atomistic-mechanical) dogma of a supposed *"social contract,"* which

---

[19] Pars. 28-29.

[20] Par. 30.

holds that society is artificially constructed by a presumed legal contract among autonomous individuals without any natural social relationships (like the artificial aggregation of atoms in Epicurean Cosmology).

Instead, following Aristotle, the later Stoics, and Thomas Aquinas, John argued that humans are *by nature social*, for they need each other and need to respect each other's rights and duties. Thus, he stated, all are called contribute to the *creation of a civic order*.[21]

Attitude of Responsibility

Once more John gestured positively in the direction of the Liberal tradition, for he said that, in the creation of this order, an individual must *enjoy freedom and be able to make up one's own mind when one acts*. But he also emphasized *authentic free will*, which goes against the grain of the implicit determinism or voluntarism with-

---

[21] Pars. 31-33. Note that this social nature of the human person is widely confirmed in the contemporary Social Sciences, but Liberal-Capitalist Economics still clings to the now discredited modern paradigm of autonomous individuals competitively making instrumentally "rational choices" based on a *utilitarian calculus of pleasure and pain*.

The American conservative writer, David Brooks, has popularized some of the Social Science research confirming this social character of human. See his helpful book, THE SOCIAL ANIMAL: THE HIDDEN SOURCES OF LOVE, CHARACTER, AND ACHIEVEMENT (New York: Random House, 2011).

Also, the neo-conservative sociologist Francis Fukuyama has pointed out this development in the Social Sciences in his interesting book, THE ORIGINS OF POLITICAL ORDER: FROM PREHUMAN TIMES TO THE FRENCH REVOLUTION (New York: Farrar, Strauss, and Giroux, 2011). See especially Chapter 2 on "The State of Nature," in which he makes clear that humans have always been social and that individualism is a "modern invention." He boldly states that Hobbes, Locke, and Hume, and also Rousseau, were all "*wrong*."

in the atomistic-mechanical understanding of freedom. So he continued:

> *The recognition of rights, observance of duties, and many-sided collaboration with other persons, should be primarily a matter of one's own personal decision, and not under the constant pressure of external coercion or enticement ... (for) society is (not) welded together by force.*[22]

Living Together in Truth, Justice, Love, & Freedom

Finally, John added a third dimension of the Catholic tradition concerning the social order, namely that the natural and free order of persons in community is *based on truth*, as well as on *justice, love,* and *freedom.*

He stated that this truth is *animated by love,* for the truth is ultimately the spiritual reality of *a true, personal, and transcendent God.* In addition, he stated that *human society thrives on freedom.*[23]

Such a society, he continued, is *founded in truth,* and must be *brought into effect by justice,* even while it seeking to preserve *freedom intact.* By so doing, he stated, society would become *increasingly more human.*[24] Further, he continued, *we must think of society as being primarily a spiritual reality.* Hence,

> *spiritual values (need to) exert a guiding influence on culture, economics, social institutions, political movements, and forms,*

---

[22] Par. 34.

[23] Pars. 35-36.

[24] Par. 36.

laws, and all other components which go to make up the exter-
nal community of persons and its continual development.[25]

A Moral Order that Has as its Basis the True God

John then declared that the ultimate foundation of such a society is
God, who is *personal and transcendent*, and *the first truth.*[26]

> *(God) is the first truth, the sovereign good, and as such the*
> *deepest source from which human society, if it is to be properly*
> *constituted, creative, and worthy of human dignity, draws its*
> *genuine vitality.*[27]

Signs of the Times:
Three Characteristics of the Present Age [28]

At the conclusion of this first substantive section, John concluded
his theory of the human order by describing what he called the
"signs of the times," which he identified as *three things which charac-*
terize our present age. These are:

---

[25] Par. 36.

[26] Pars. 37-38

[27] Par. 38.

[28] The English text refers to *the modern age,* but the Latin text refers, in a literal
translation, to *this our age* (*Aetas haec nostra*) and does not use the term *modern.*
Also, in a gross omission, the English text leaves out entirely the heading *Signs*
of the Times.

- **Gains of the Working Class.** First, he pointed to the self-emancipation of the working class, initially by achieving socio-economic rights, then political rights, and now cultural rights.

- **Women in Public Life.** Second, he pointed to the growing entry of women into public life, as they demand their rights and duties in both domestic and public spheres, according to their natural dignity, and especially in the Christian nations.

- **Defeat of Colonialism.** Third, he pointed to the fact that nations formerly suffering under colonial domination had struggled for, and won, their political independence [29]

In his summary of these three signs of the times, John declared:

> *Thus all over the world humans are either the citizens of an independent State, or are shortly to become so; nor is any nation nowadays content to submit to foreign domination. The long-standing inferiority complex of certain classes because of their economic and social status, sex, or position in the State, and the corresponding superiority complex of other classes, is rapidly becoming a thing of the past.*[30]

Adding the racial dimension, central to Western colonialism, John enjoined:

> *Today, on the contrary the conviction is widespread that all humans are equal in dignity; and so, on the doctrinal and theo-*

---

[29] Pars. 39-42.

[30] Par. 43.

retical level at least, no form of approval is being given to racial discrimination.[31]

---

[31] Par. 44.

PART II

RELATIONSHIPS BETWEEN

HUMAN BEINGS & PUBLIC AUTHORITIES

WITHIN INDIVIDUAL POLITICAL COMMUNITIES

Necessity of Authority & its Divine Origin

I n the second major section of PACEM IN TERRIS, John addressed the relationship of human beings to political authority within individual political communities. Such authorities, he wrote, have the task of preserving the institutions of social order and of aiding the interests of its members, and they derive their authority from God. But, he stated, this God-given authority is not a voluntaristic one deserving blind obedience. Rather, its nature is to be a rational and hence purposeful authority.[32] He appealed to an earlier classic statement by Pope Leo XIII (1878-1903):

> God has created humans as social by nature, and a society can-
> not hold together unless someone is in command to give effec-
> tive direction and unity of purpose. Hence every civilized com-
> munity must have a ruling authority, and this authority, no

---

[32] Par. 46.

*less than society itself, has its source in nature, and consequent-
ly has God for its author.*[33]

Such authority, John stated, needs to *govern in accordance with right
reason.* By contrast, he argued,

> *a regime which governs solely or mainly by means of threats
> and intimidation or promises of reward, provides human beings
> with no incentive to work for the common good.*[34]

For this reason, he stated that *the appeal of rulers should be to the
individual conscience;* for *no human being has the capacity to force individual compliance on another ... Only God can do that.* Further, he
continued, *laws passed in contravention of the moral order, and hence of
the divine will, can have no binding force in conscience.* Then he noted
that *all this teaching is consonant with any genuinely democratic form of
government.*[35]

John was clearly defending *democracy,* and he was critiquing both
communist and fascist forms of *dictatorship.*

Implementation of the Common Good:
The Reason for Government to Exist

All humans, he stated, both individually and in intermediate
groups, need to contribute to the common good. They need to
harmonize their interests with the needs of others. Those who govern need to exercise their authority for the common good. Thus,

---

[33] Par. 46.

[34] Par. 48

[35] Pars. 46-52.

26

the very reason for the existence of government, John continued, is *the attainment of the common good*. Again, individuals in turn need to *harmonize their own interests with the needs of others*, and so those in authority must exercise that authority in a way *best calculated* to promote this common good.[36]

Fundamental Aspects of the Common Good

Included within the common good, John continued, are the *characteristics distinctive of each individual people*, but ultimately the common good is based on the human nature and the human person. He then stated that *it is in the nature of the common good that every single citizen has the right to share in it – although in different ways*.[37]

Further, he insisted that

> *justice and equity can at times argue that those in power pay more attention to the weaker members of society, since these are at a disadvantage when it comes to defending their own rights and asserting their legitimate interests.*[38]

Every citizen, he said, has the right to share in the common good, with the result that sometimes justice and equity demand that *those in authority pay more attention to the weaker members of society*.[39]

The common good, he added, must also take into account the whole human person, body and soul, *according to the hierarchy of*

---

36 Pars. 53-54.

37 Pars. 55-56.

38 Pars. 56.

39 Pars. 53-59.

27

values. Thus authorities are responsible, he declared, for *the spiritual as well as the material prosperity of their citizens.*[40]

Responsibilities of Public Power &
Rights & Duties of the Person

Today, John reported, *the common good is best safeguarded when personal rights and duties are guaranteed.* Hence safeguarding human rights and facilitating human duties, as well as their *superintendence and coordination,* is *the principle duty of every public authority.* For this reason, the decrees of any government which refuses to recognize human rights, or which violates them, *would be wholly lacking in binding force.*[41]

Harmonizing & Protecting
the Rights & Duties of the Person

A principle duty of government, John continued, is to guard and coordinate persons' rights in society. This requires not suppressing individual rights, and not allowing any citizens to obstruct the rights of other citizens. It also requires restoring rights where they have been violated.[42]

Duty of Promoting the Rights of Persons

John also stated that the government needs to create a climate favorable to the rights of the person. Otherwise, as we have learned, *in the modern world, political, economic, and cultural inequities among*

---

[40] Pars. 57-59.

[41] Pars. 60-61.

[42] Par. 62.

citizens become more and more widespread. Such promotion of human rights includes *the question of social as well as economic progress,* and *the development of essential services* (e.g., *road-building, transportation, communications, drinking-water, housing, medical care,* etc.), as well as

> *the provision of insurance facilities, to obviate any likelihood of a citizen's being unable to maintain a decent standard of living in the event of some misfortune, and or greatly increased family responsibilities.*[43]

Further, the government is required to work on behalf of opportunities for *suitable employment* and to defend *a just and equitable wage.* It should also *facilitate the formation of intermediate groups,* and the sharing in cultural benefits, and to ensure that all share in *cultural benefits.*[44]

Balance between Two Forms of Intervention

Next John noted that indicated that a careful balance is required between defending and promoting individual rights. Thus, even given an *extensive and far-reaching influence of the State on the economy,* the State should never *deprive individual citizens of their freedom of action.*[45]

Structure & Function of Public Power

While it is not possible to make a general rule about the best form of government, John maintained, it seems best that the state em-

---

[43] Pars. 63-64.

[44] Par. 64.

[45] Pars. 65-66.

body *a three-fold division of public office,* namely the *legislative, administrative, and judicial functions.* In all of this the *moral law* and the *common good* must be respected, and *justice* must be *the guiding principle.* This requires, for example, that j*ustice must be administered impartially* and that *judges must be wholly incorrupt and uninfluenced by the solicitations of interested parties.* Similarly, both *individuals and intermediate groups* need to be protected in their rights.[46]

Legal Order & Moral Consciousness

Because of the complexity of contemporary life, John declared, states need to *adapt the laws to the conditions of modern life and seek solutions to new problems.* But today change often happens so fast and in such a complex manner that the law sometimes seems inadequate. So governments, while understanding their limits, need *to recognize at once what is needed in a given situation, and act with promptness and efficiency.*[47]

Participation of Citizens in Public Life

Because of the dignity of human beings, he said, they have an unquestionable *right to take an active part in government,* though the degree may vary with the *stage of development.* In this context, he stated that government service *takes on a new vitality.*

Signs of the Times

At the present time, John declared, John continued, these ideas are best realized by, first, *a clear and precisely worded charter of funda-*

---

[46] Pars. 68-69.

[47] Pars. 70-72.

mental human rights ... formulated and incorporated into the State's general constitutions. Secondly, he stated, *each state must have a public constitution.* And third, *relations between citizens and public authorities (must) be described in terms of rights and duties.*[48]

John then rejected *the view that the will of the individual or of the group is the primary and only source of a citizen's rights and duties.* This explains, he stated, the contemporary demand for *constitutional recognition* of *inviolable rights,* as well as *observance of constitutional procedures.*[49]

(Seeing human rights only in a *voluntarist* perspective in which they are simply the result of human will – be it of the individual or the state – is a logical corollary of the *atomistic-mechanical* philosophical Cosmology.)

---

[48] Pars. 75-77.
[49] Pars. 76-79.

PART III

RELATIONSHIPS AMONG

POLITICAL COMMUNITIES

Subjects of Rights and Duties

I n this third substantive section of this encyclical, John affirmed that *the same law of nature that governs the life and conduct of individuals must also govern the relations of political communities* among themselves. Such reciprocal relationships, he stated, are essential to society and they are bound by the common good and the moral order, which the Creator has inscribed in every heart.[50]

In Truth

These relationships among nations, John continued, need to be guided first of all by truth, which *calls for the elimination of every trace of racial discrimination* and *recognition of the inviolable principle that all states are by nature equal in dignity*. Further, he wrote, each state has the right to exist and to develop, with a *primary responsibility for its own development*.[51]

---

[50] Pars. 80-85.

[51] Par. 86

No nation, even if superior in development, may *exert unjust domination over other nations.* Rather, more developed nations should make *a greater contribution to the common cause of social progress.* Further, and apparently describing false propaganda, John stated that there should be no dissemination of information which violates *the principles of truth and justice, and injures the reputation of another nation.*[52]

According to Justice

Relations between states, John declared, should be regulated by *justice,* including recognition of *mutual rights* and *respective duties* (e.g., the right to exist, to development, to good name and honor, as well as the correlative duties). He cited Augustine's famous statement that the government of kingdoms without justice is nothing more than a *band of robbers.* Clashes of interest among states, he continued, should be resolved *neither by armed force nor by deceit or trickery,* but by an *objective investigation* and an *equitable reconciliation.*[53]

Treatment of Minorities

Minority peoples, John stated, while they cannot always live in a separate nation, should be allowed vitality and growth, including protection of *language, culture, ancient traditions, and economic activity and enterprise.* These minority peoples in turn should enter into cooperative association with those with whom they live.[54]

---

[52] Pars. 87-90.

[53] Pars. 91-93.

[54] Pars. 94-97.

Active Solidarity

John affirmed that states should take *positive steps to pool their material and spiritual resources,* for the common good of the state *cannot be divorced from the common good of the entire human family.* Reciprocal relations must be allowed among intermediate groups within states, including ethnic groups.[55]

Proper Balance among
Population, Land, and Capital

Then John insisted that, where there are economic imbalances in some countries, other countries should help in the *circulation of goods, capital, and manpower.* Wherever possible, work should be brought to the workers, particularly to *agricultural workers.*[56]

> *We advocate in such cases the policy of bringing the work to the workers, wherever possible, rather than bringing workers to the scene of the work ... without being exposed to the painful necessity of uprooting themselves from their own homes, settling in a strange environment, and forming new social contacts.*[57]

The Problem of Political Refugees

John stated that he personally felt a *bitter anguish of spirit (toward) the plight of those who for political reasons have been exiled from their own homelands.* Refugees are persons, he insisted, who do not lose their rights *simply because they are deprived of citizenship.* He wrote

---

[55] Pars. 98-100,

[56] Pars. 101-102.

[57] Par. 102.

of the *great numbers* and *incredible suffering* of these refugees. He argued that national leaders had been *too restrictive* with immigration policies, and that the denial of true freedom to these refugees represented *a complete reversal of the right order of society ... (and of) the whole raison d'être of political authority.* These refugees are human persons with the rights of human citizenship. Nations should accept such immigrants, *so far as the good of their own community, rightly understood, permits.*[58]

Disarmament

In this section, John highlighted what for him constituted the most serious issue of relations among states, namely the arms race and the need for disarmament. While *the principles of human solidarity or Christian charity should guide the relations among states in helping each other,* John saw instead

> *the enormous stocks of armaments ... manufactured in the economically more developed countries ... in turn involving a vast outlay of intellectual and material resources.*[59]

In addition, he wrote that as a result of this arms race

> *the people of these countries are saddled with a great burden, while other countries lack the help they need for their economic and social development.*[60]

---

[58] Pars. 103-108.

[59] Par. 109.

[60] Par. 109.

John decried the *erroneous belief* that peace could be assured only by *an equal balance of armaments,* and particularly of *atomic weapons.* He saw such weapons as causing people to live in *the grip of constant fear* of *an impending storm* of *horrific violence.*[61]

Even if the holding of such armaments did act as a deterrent, John warned ecologically that *"the very testing of nuclear devices for war purposes can, if continued, lead to serious danger for various forms of life on Earth."*[62] (This may be the first significant reference in the modern corpus of papal encyclicals to a *global ecological danger* threatening all forms of life.)

When referring to nuclear weapons, John used apocalyptic language: *constant fear ... impending storm ... appalling slaughter and destruction ... conflagration ...monstrous power.* He demanded that the arms race cease, that stockpiles be reduced, that nuclear weapons be banned, and that there be negotiated a general agreement of disarmament.[63]

To be complete, he wrote, such disarmament must *reach human beings' very souls.* He then repeated his earlier point:

> *The fundamental principles upon which peace is based in today's world (need to be) be replaced by an altogether different one, namely, the realization that true and lasting peace among nations cannot consist in the possession of an equal supply of*

---

[61] Pars. 110-111.

[62] Pars. 110-111.

[63] Par. 111.

armaments but only in mutual trust. And we are confident that this can be achieved.[64]

Finally, John the identified three fundamental grounds for disarmament: 1) the demand of *reason*; 2) the *craving of people* for it; and 3) the *rich possibilities for good* which could flow from it. In the name of Jesus Christ and of all humankind, he begged and beseeched especially *the rulers of states* to seek this path. He told his readers that he would *pray unceasingly* for this cause.[65]

In Liberty

Building on his call for disarmament, John called for *relations between states* to be guided by *the principle of freedom*. He pleaded that there be no oppression of one country by another, and that the wealthier states come to the aid of the poorer states, so that there would be born a new order founded on *freedom, integrity, and security*.[66]

Rise of Political Communities in
the Process of Economic Development

John declared that all human beings are united by their common origin and are called to form *one common Christian family*. He recalled the appeal in his earlier encyclical, MATER ET MAGISTRA, to *the wealthier nations to render every kind of assistance to states which are still in the process of economic development*.[67]

---

[64] Pars. 112-113.

[65] Pars. 114-119.

[66] Par. 120.

He then cited a large quote from his predecessor, Pope Pius XII:

> *A new order founded on moral principles is the surest bulwark against the violation of the freedom, integrity and security of other nations, no matter what may be their territorial extension or their capacity for defense.*

> *For although it is almost inevitable that the larger States, in view of their greater power and vaster resources, will themselves decide on the norms governing their economic associations with small States, nevertheless these smaller States cannot be denied their right, in keeping with the common good, to political freedom, and to the adoption of a position of neutrality in the conflicts between nations.*

> *No State can be denied this right, for it is a postulate of the Natural Law itself, as also of international law. These smaller States have also the right of assuring their own economic development.*

> *It is only with the effective guaranteeing of these rights that smaller nations can fittingly promote the common good of all mankind, as well as the material welfare and the cultural and spiritual progress of their own people.*[68]

The wealthier states, he continued, must *repudiate any policy of domination,* and instead provide assistance to them. In doing so, they

---

[67] Pars. 121-123.

[68] Par. 124. The source is Pius XII's 1941 Christmas radio message.

will make *a precious contribution ... to the formation of a world community.*[69]

Signs of the Times

Concluding this section, John rejoiced that today people wish to solve disputes among states peaceably and avoid war, mainly because of the great destructiveness of atomic weapons. Yet, he stated, *fear* prevails and leads nations *to spend enormous sums on armaments.* So he warmly urged leaders to come together to seek a peace based *on our common human nature,* so that *love, not fear, (might) dominate the relationships among individuals and among nations.*

He then repeated his call for disarmament negotiations, and insisted that *in this age that boasts of atomic power, it no longer make sense to maintain that war is a fit instrument with which to repair the violation of justice.* Instead, he expressed his proclamation that *love, not fear, must dominate the relationships between individuals and between nations.*[70]

---

[69] Par. 125.

[70] Pars. 126-129.

PART IV

RELATIONSHIPS OF HUMAN BEINGS
AND POLITICAL COMMUNITIES WITH
THE WORLD COMMUNITY

Interdependence
among Political Communities

J ohn opened this fourth and briefer section of his encyclical by declaring that a new *world economy* is now been born:

> *Progress in science and technology ... has led to a phenomenal growth in relationships among individuals, families and intermediate associations belonging to the various nations, and among the public authorities of the various political communities. There is also a growing economic interdependence among States. National economies are gradually becoming so interdependent that a kind of **world economy** is being born from the simultaneous integration of the economies of individual States. And finally, each country's social progress, order, security and peace are necessarily linked with the social progress, order, security and peace of every other country.*[71] (Bold font added.)

For this reason, he wrote:

---

[71] Par. 130.

No State can fittingly pursue its own interests in isolation from the rest, nor, under such circumstances, can it develop itself as it should. The prosperity and progress of any State is in part consequence, and in part cause, of the prosperity and progress of all other States.[72]

Failure of Political Authority
Regarding the Universal Common Good

In the past, John noted, *rulers of States* worked out their relationships by means of *diplomatic channels* and *top-level meetings and discussions, treaties, and agreements.* But in our day, he argued, the *gravity, urgency, and complexity* of problems, and especially *the preservation of the security and peace of the whole world,* prove that individual nations on an equal footing, were unable alone to resolve these problems.[73]

So John logically and solemnly judged that

we are thus driven to the conclusion that the shape and structure of political life in the contemporary world, and the influence exercised by public authority in all the nations of the world are unequal to the task of promoting the common good of all peoples.[74]

---

[72] Par. 131.

[73] Pars. 132-134.

[74] Par. 135.

Relationship of the Historical Content
of the Common Good & the Structure and Function
of Public Power

John then argued that the common good by its nature requires *a public authority* as *a postulate of the moral order*. But, he continued, to be effective it requires a certain structure capable of realizing its goal in the face of changing historical conditions.[75] Reflecting then on contemporary *historical conditions,* especially the rise of a *global economy,* John made the dramatic endorsement of a *global political authority* commensurate with the new global economy:

> *Today the universal common good presents us with problems which are world-wide in their dimensions; problems, therefore, which cannot be solved except by **a public authority** with power, organization and means co-extensive with these problems, and **with a world-wide sphere of activity.** Consequently the moral order itself demands the establishment of some such general form of public authority.*[76] (Bold font added.)

Public Authority Instituted by Common Agreement
& Not Imposed by Force

John stated that this global public authority should be set up by *consensus* among nations, not by *force,* and that it should be guided by the common good and personal rights.[77]

---

[75] Par. 136.

[76] Par. 137.

[77] Pars. 138.

Universal Common Good
& the Rights of the Person

This authority, John continued, should have the special mission of guarding both the *rights of the human person* and t*he common good of all states*, either through *direct action* or by establishing *supportive conditions*.[78]

Principle of Subsidiarity

John then raised the principle of subsidiarity, which requires that government support and not displace the roles of individuals, families, and intermediate associations. Similarly, he argued, a global authority should support and not displace the public authority of individual states.[79]

Signs of the Times

Concluding this section, John highlighted the *United Nations Organization* (UN), established in 1945, and its specialized member agencies. He noted its special aim of *maintaining and strengthening peace*, and he hailed its *Universal Declaration of Human Rights* approved by its General Assembly in 1948. While acknowledging that there were some reservations about the Declaration, he described it *as a step in the right direction, an approach toward the establishment of a juridical and political ordering of the world community*.[80]

He then called for *adaptation and expansion* of the role of the UN:

---

[78] Par. 139.

[79] Pars. 140-141.

[80] Pars. 141-144.

It is therefore Our earnest wish that the United Nations Organ-
ization may be able progressively to adapt its structure and me-
thods of operations to the magnitude and nobility of its tasks.[81]

Here, John was asking that the UN evolve into a structure of *global governance* commensurate in scale with the new world-economy, in response to this new historical moment when *human beings are becoming more and more conscious of being living members of a world community.*[82]

---

[81] Par. 145.

[82] Par. 145.

PART V

PASTORAL REFERENCES

Duty to Participate in Public Life

I n this final section of PACEM IN TERRIS, John exhorted all Catholics to become active in public life for the sake of the common good of the human family and for their own political communities. This is a mandate, he stated, of their Christian faith, *with love as the guide.*[83]

Scientific Expertise, Technical Skills, Professional Experience

In order to *imbue Civilization with right ideals and Christian principles,* John then urged Catholics to *influence social institutions* and to do so *effectively from within* by means of scientific, technical, and professional competence.[84]

---

[83] Par. 146.

[84] Pars. 147-148.

Action as a Synthesis of Scientific-Technical
& Professional Elements with Spiritual Values

While repeating his insistence on scientific-technical competence and professional experience, John added the need to integrate these with the laws of *nature*, with *precepts of the moral order*, with *human reason*, and ultimately with *spiritual values*.[85]

Reuniting in Believers Religious Faith
& Historical Awareness

John lamented that in today's advanced scientific-technological societies, many believers do not bring their faith to bear on the *creation of institutions*. This is due, he proposed, to a *cleavage between faith and practice*. The solution, he argued, is to restore the *inner spiritual unity* which makes *faith ... the motivating force of action*. This influence must be guided by *the precepts of the moral order*, follow *the providential designs of God*, and integrate *spiritual values with those of science, technology and the professions*.[86]

Integral Development of
Human Beings in Formation

The reason for this *divorce between faith and practice*, John claimed, was *an inadequate formation in Christian teaching and Christian morality*. Hence the answer was better formation in this area.[87]

---

[85] Pars. 149-150.

[86] Pars. 151-152.

[87] Par. 153.

Scientific training reaches a very high level, whereas religious training generally does not advance beyond the elementary stage. It is essential, therefore, that the education given to our young people be holistic and continuous, and imparted in such a way that moral goodness and the cultivation of religious values may keep pace with scientific knowledge and continually advancing technical progress.[88]

Continuous Commitment

Then John noted the difficulty of this challenge:

How difficult it is to understand clearly the relation between the objective requirements of justice and concrete situations; to define, that is, correctly to what degree and in what form doctrinal principles and directives must be applied in the given state of human society.[89]

For this reason, John urged all Catholic Christians not to be *satisfied with what they have achieved.* Rather, he continued, all human professions – *industry, trade unions, professional organizations, insurance, cultural institutions, the law, politics, medical and recreational facilities, and other such activities* – need to take up the challenge. This all the more urgent, he declared, since our age has *discovered the atom and achieved the breakthrough into outer space.*[90]

---

[88] Par. 153.

[89] Par. 154.

[90] Pars. 155-156.

Relationship of Catholics & Non-Catholics
In the Economic-Social-Political Field

In this new task, John called for *extensive cooperation between Catholics and those Christians who are separated from this Apostolic See.* He also called for *the cooperation of Catholics with persons who may not be Christians but who nevertheless are reasonable persons, and persons of natural moral integrity.* In such encounters, he added, while nothing should be done to compromise religion and morality, they should be *animated by a spirit of spirit of understanding and unselfishness, ready to co-operate loyally in achieving objects which are good in themselves, or conducive to good.*[91]

Distinguishing between Error Itself
& Persons in Error

Continuing in this line, John made his now famous distinction *between error as such and the person who falls into error.* This distinction provided his justification for ecumenical dialogue and cooperation with non-Catholic Christians, for interfaith dialogue and cooperation, and even for dialogue and cooperation with Marxists, including secular socialists and atheistic communists. John's reason for making this distinction is that the person in error never loses human dignity and also, if approached in dialogue, may come to the truth.[92]

So dramatic was this change in official Catholic policy that it may be helpful to cite John's own words at length.

---

[91] Par. 157.

[92] Par. 158.

It is always perfectly justifiable to distinguish between error as such and the person who falls into error – even in the case of persons who err regarding the truth or are led astray as a result of their inadequate knowledge, in matters either of religion or of the highest ethical standards.

A person who has fallen into error does not cease to be a person. Such a one never forfeits personal dignity, and that must always be taken into account.

Besides, there exists in the human being's very nature an undying capacity to break through the barriers of error and seek the road to truth. God, in His great providence, is ever present with His aid.

Today, maybe, a person lacks faith and turns aside into error; tomorrow, perhaps, illumined by God's light, the person may indeed embrace the truth.[93]

John then continued:

Catholics who, in order to achieve some external good, collaborate with unbelievers or with anyone who through error lacks the fullness of faith in Christ, may possibly provide the occasion or even the incentive for their conversion to the truth.[94]

Once more, John emphasized his point:

---

[93] Par. 158.

[94] Par. 158.

Again, it is perfectly legitimate to make a clear distinction be-
tween a false Philosophy of the nature, origin and purpose of
humans and the world, and economic, social, cultural, and po-
litical undertakings, even when such undertakings draw their
origin and inspiration from that Philosophy.

True, the philosophic formula does not change once it has been
set down in precise terms, but the undertakings clearly cannot
avoid being influenced to a certain extent by the changing con-
ditions in which they have to operate.

Besides, who can deny the possible existence of good and com-
mendable elements in these undertakings, elements which do
indeed conform to the dictates of right reason, and are an ex-
pression of humanity's lawful aspirations.[95]

Such cooperation, John noted, should be guided by *prudence*, with
those Catholics who take a leading part in the life of the community and
in these specific fields making the judgment, though in conformity
with *the Church's social teaching and the directives of ecclesiastical au-*
thority.[96]

With a few words from his pen, John suddenly and dramatically
reversed a central plank of Catholic strategy since the time of Pope
Leo XIII.

John also reversed as the *official Catholic hostility* since the Reforma-
tion against *Protestant Christians,* and since the Middle Ages
against *Orthodox Christians.*

---

[95] Par. 159.

[96] Par. 160.

52

Most dramatic was John's reversal of the once *official ban* on Catholic dialogue or cooperation with *socialists or communists*. He had long ago broken beyond this ban in his own life. Now he made it official for the entire Catholic Church.

In that regard, Catholics were suddenly and officially free to dialogue and to cooperate with socialists and communists, even while not accepting their ideologies. Further, despite the errors of these ideologies, Catholics could still recognize good in them. Finally, as John had stated, such cooperation could also be an occasion of conversion for those in error.

John thus negated the core anti-socialist element of the Catholic strategy designed at the close of the 19th century by Pope Leo XIII.

Gradually

John again reminded his readers that, if gains are to be made in this area, they will have to be done gradually. For that, he said, is a law of nature. Real change, he argued, comes only from working slowly within institutions. The alternative, he stated, is a disharmony that leaves ruin in its wake.[97]

An Immense Task

Further, John described the immensity of the task *to create world peace,* and he noted that those who labor on its behalf are *few.* But he was encouraged by the hope that more would join the cause, especially Christians who are called to be *a leaven of love in the*

---

[97] Pars. 161-162.

world. He then reminded his readers that true peace is from God, who is the source of all order.[98]

Conclusion:
The Prince of Peace

John concluded his encyclical with an appeal to *the Prince of Peace*, and he prayed that Christ would *inflame the desires of all persons to break through the barriers which divide them*. He also urged his brother bishops to show special care for *those who are most lowly and in the greatest need of help and defense*.[99]

---

[98] Pars. 163-165.

[99] Pars. 166-171.

CONCLUDING REFLECTION

ON THE ENCYCLICAL

P ACEM IN TERRIS was issued on Holy Thursday, 11 April 1963, less than two months before John's death. Even as he worked on it, cancer was eating away at his body. This was John's last and greatest encyclical letter.

Strategic Shift in Catholic Social Teaching

In this encyclical, John *dramatically shifted the institutional strategy of Catholic Social Teaching* from its long-lasting but no longer success-ful Leonine stage (that is, since Pope Leo XIII who died in 1903). In the wide range of this strategic shift – as seen in John's writings and actions – he accepted the *apertura a sinestra* (opening to the left) both within the capitalist countries and in relation to Social-ism and Communism.

John also encouraged Christian *ecumenism*, reconciliation with *Ju-daism*, and broad *interfaith* dialogue and cooperation. In addition, he permitted an expansion of theological life beyond the tradition-al neo-scholastic framework. Further, John no longer limited Catholic support to confessional political parties.

Most importantly, John broadened Social Catholicism from its Leonine focus on *Catholic workers and employers in the industrialized countries* to a wide range of global social questions touching *all of humanity.* In addition, he embraced *human rights,* and sought for them deeper philosophical grounding. And he placed special emphasis on *agriculture and agricultural workers,* in what may be described as his *agro-ecological vision.*

In sum, John shifted the official Catholic strategic framework to the pluralistic, post-colonial, post-ideological vision of an emerging *Global Civilization* and of an emerging *World Church,* with the latter as the humble and loving servant of the former. In his dying statement, John reaffirmed this shift of church strategy from service of Catholics to service of all humanity, and from defense of the rights of the Catholic Church to defense of the rights of the human person. He expanded the Catholic Church's self-understanding from defending a non-historical *deposit of faith* to the historically evolutionary task of *reading the signs of the times.*

Because of the brevity of his papacy and the limits of his knowledge at the time, John only pointed toward this fresh postmodern global strategic direction. It would remain for his successors to attempt to define and implement the Johannine strategy in its full institutional and societal implications – something that would prove not an easy task.

Nonetheless, I propose that John's person, actions, writings, and especially his two major social encyclicals MATER ET MAGISTRA and PACEM IN TERRIS, as well as his Ecumenical Council Vatican II, all constitute *the prophetic foundation for a postmodern Johannine Catholic strategy* in which the emerging *World Church* is called to humble and loving service of the emerging *Global Civilization.*

ABOUT THE AUTHOR

JOE HOLLAND, an eco-social philosopher and Catholic theologian, holds a Ph.D. in Theology in the field of Social Ethics from the University of Chicago, and he was a Fulbright Scholar in Philosophy at the *Universidad Católica* in Santiago, Chile. Currently, he is Professor of Philosophy & Religion at Saint Thomas University in Miami Gardens, Florida; Permanent Visiting Professor at the *Universidad Nacional del Altiplano* in Puno, Peru; a frequent lecturer at the *Universidad Mayor de*

San Andrés in La Paz, Bolivia; President of Pacem in Terris Global Leadership Initiative and of Pax Romana/Cmica-usa; co-founder and Vice-Chair of Catholic Scholars for Worker Justice; a member of the Catholic Labor Network; and a member of the International Association for Catholic Social Thought, based at the University of Leuven in Belgium.

Earlier, Joe served as an Associate at the Center of Concern, an internationally oriented social-justice "think tank" in Washington DC jointly founded by the international Jesuit order and the U.S. Catholic Bishops. While at the Center, he co-founded the National Conference on Religion and Labor, co-sponsored by the AFL-CIO, and he also founded the American Catholic Lay Network. Later, he served as founding Director of the Pallottine Institute for Lay Leadership and Research at Seton Hall University in South Orange, New Jersey. In addition, he was the principal consultant-writer for the 1975 pastoral letter from the 25 Catholic bishops of Appalachia, THIS LAND IS HOME TO ME, and for the bishops 1995 sequel pastoral document AT HOME IN THE WEB OF LIFE.

Also, Joe has lectured at Georgetown, Harvard, Notre Dame, Princeton, and other universities in the United States, as well as at the *Institut Catholique* in Paris, France, Sogang University in Seoul, Korea, Sophia University in Tokyo, Japan, the Pontifical Catholic University in São Paulo, Brazil, and other universities across the world. In 1986 he was given the Isaac Hecker Award for Social Justice, and in 2002 he was awarded the Athena Medal of Excellence by the *Universidad Nacional del Altiplano* in Peru. He is married to Paquita Biascoechea-Martinez, a native of Puerto Rico, and they have two children and four grandchildren.

THE PACEM IN TERRIS

GLOBAL LEADERSHIP INITIATIVE

 The Pacem in Terris Initiative, whose full name is the *Pacem in Terris Global Leadership Intellectual-Artistic Ecumenical Initiative*, fosters local-global intellectual-spiritual research and dialogue on behalf of a *Postmodern Global Christian Intellectual-Artistic Renaissance.*

This Postmodern Renaissance is seen as helping to guide the global human family, and within it the global Christian family, out of *the traumatic breakdown of Modern Western Industrial-Colonial Civilization* (now globalized) and out of *the equally traumatic breakdown of the Modern Western Catholic Industrial-Colonial Paradigm of Evangelization* (also globalized). It also seeks to help guide the global human family and the global Christian family toward *a regenerative Postmodern Local-Global Electronic-Ecological Civilization* and toward *a regenerative Postmodern Local-Global Electronic-Ecological "New Evangelization."*

The Initiative's service of the emerging Global Christian Renaissance is grounded intellectually, artistically, and spiritually in the two books of Divine Revelation, namely *the sacred Book of Nature and the sacred Book of the Bible*, in *postmodern global strategy of Catholic Social Teaching* founded by Pope John XXIII, and in the emerging postmodern philosophical-scientific *"New Cosmology."* To launch the Initiative, Pax Romana / Cmica-usa issued in early 2012 to Protestant, Orthodox, and Catholic Christians across the world a public *"Ecumenical Invitation"* to join this local-global process of dialogue and study. It also issued an *"Initial Working Document"* and a *"Reflection Paper on Cosmology and Hope."* All of these documents may be located on the Pacem in Terris Initiative's website at www.paceminterris.net.

To provide ongoing intellectual resources for the Initiative, Pax Romana / Cmica-usa has created a new publishing arm for the Initiative, namely *Pacem in Terris Press*. This Press will soon published a collection of all of the Initiative's initial documents, as well as a study of the postmodern vision of Blessed John XXIII. Also, interested scholars are invited to submit for consideration by the Press well-researched and well-written manuscripts related to the work of the Initiative. For more information, contact paceminterris@comcast.net.

ADDITIONAL COPIES OF THIS BOOK

"PACEM IN TERRIS"

Summary & Commentary for the 50th Anniversary

of the Famous Encyclical Letter of

Pope John XXIII on World Peace

US $8.95, Paperback, 59 Pages

ISBN-13: 978-1479126347

ISBN-10: 1479126349

ORDER ONLINE FROM

https://www.createspace.com/3965543

Copy the above link into your browser.
Then click on the "ADD TO CART" button under book cover.
Note that this secure link begins with "https" and NOT "http."
The "s" at the end indicates it is a secure link.
"https://" needs to be entered before "www."

CPSIA information can be obtained at www.ICGtesting.com
Printed in the USA
LVOW10s1921030715

444905LV00001B/25/P